Bookends

A play

Scott Perry

Samuel French—London
New York-Toronto-Hollywood

BOOKENDS

First produced at the Man in the Moon Theatre, Chelsea,
on 15th August 1995, with the following cast:

Bill	Kevin Laffan
Ron	Ken Ratcliffe

Director Olly Lambert
Lighting Colin Wilson

CHARACTERS

Bill, *seventy*
Ron, *seventy*

The action of the play takes place on a park bench late in the afternoon on a day in late autumn

Time: the present

In memory of David

BOOKENDS

A park bench

Late autumn. Late afternoon

When the play begins, two old men, Bill and Ron, are sitting on the bench. Both men wear overcoats. Ron is wearing a bright new pair of basketball boots. Of the two he is the more self-centred, egotistical, and brash. Bill is wearing old, well made, black leather shoes. Of the two he is the more thoughtful, quiet and circumspect

Ron Where were you? I came here at five o'clock; I thought "If he's going to be anywhere at five o'clock, he's going to be here."

Bill No. I wasn't here.

Ron I know that, I could see that, couldn't I? I'm not a fool. I waited though.

Bill Oh well.

Ron What happened to our five o'clock spot?

Bill I wasn't here.

Ron I know that.

Bill You didn't tell me you were coming, did you?

Ron It was a surprise. I was going to creep up on you.

Bill No good if I'm not here.

Ron I scared the life out of some poor bugger.

Bill Well, it wasn't me.

Ron I could see that. Haven't you been at all?

Bill Of course I've been.

Ron Not yesterday.

Bill I'm here today, aren't I?

Ron Well?

Bill Well what?

Ron Where were you?

Bill I was away.

Ron What on earth for?

Bill Because I was.

Ron I felt a right idiot.

Bill Well, I went away.

Ron What about our five o'clock spot?

Bill What about it?

Ron I just thought you'd be here, that's all.

Bill Ron, *you* haven't been here for *three weeks*. I didn't know, did I? There's no point in going to a meeting place if there's no one to meet. What do I want to sit here on my own for?

Ron Why did you come here now then?

Bill Because I felt like it.

Ron Felt like it.

Bill It's your fault for going away in the first place.

Ron What's my fault?

Bill I don't have to come here.

Ron Where else is there to go?

Bill There are lots of places. Stay at home for a start.

Ron You weren't at home.

Bill How do you know?

Ron Because I rang.

Pause

Bill No, I was in Scarborough.

Ron (*after a beat*) Well, *I'm* back.

Bill Not before time.

Ron Oh yes, straight out, Bill.

Bill I thought you would.

Ron Course I would. You're shocked, aren't you? You didn't
expect it, you didn't expect to see me back here so soon — well
I can tell you I was waltzing, Bill, I was waltzing down the street.

Bill Did they try and stop you?

Ron Did they hell.

Bill But they must have said something.

Ron (*confidentially*)They didn't know.

Bill You're joking.

Ron They knew nothing.

Bill They must have seen you.

Ron Toilet window, Bill, toilet window. I took my bag of essentials
and climbed out, it was as easy as that. Oh, yes.

Bill (*excitedly*)You sly old bastard.

Ron I know what's good for me.

Bill You bloody sly old bastard.

Ron No one gives me the run-around. I had to get out. Had to,
couldn't stand it any longer.

Bill I don't blame you.

Ron No?

Bill Don't blame you, I've been to those places myself.

Ron When?

Bill Once or twice.

Ron When?

Bill Plenty of times. Visiting.

Ron It's not a holiday camp.

Bill Visiting people, you know what I mean.

Ron Didn't visit me.

Bill No.

Ron Bloody swine, in there — full of swine. They're going to come
looking for me.

Bill How long've you been out?

Ron Couple of days. I came here yesterday, you weren't here.

Bill They'll have you on the missing persons list.

Ron They'll be looking for me.

Bill What are you going to do?

Ron Let them look. Let them sweat it out a bit.

Pause

I've been home. They haven't sold it. Still got the keys, you see, Bill.

Bill That's the first place they'll go.

Ron I've moved to a bed and breakfast for now.

Bill You bugger.

Ron Well.

Bill You'll have to go back sometime.

Ron Yeah, but let them wonder first, let them stew over what's happened to me.

Bill Is that wise, Ron?

Ron Well, I want something done. I want a bloody scene so they know, I want them to know. I'll shake them up a bit. I should never have been sent, I should never have gone. I'm not an old fart, not yet. They bamboozled me, that's all. That's all they did.

Bill Yeah, well.

Ron Well, they did, didn't they?

Bill Not really.

Ron Yes, they did.

Bill I don't know.

Ron They bamboozled me.

Bill No.

Ron They bamboozled me.

Bill I think you brought it on yourself.

Ron looks at Bill

Yes you did.

Ron Rubbish.

Bill You went away and disappeared, just like you have this time, you let everyone worry about you ——

Ron What I do is my business.

Bill Just like you did when you caused all the trouble in the first place.

Ron You knew where I was going, you could have come with me then.

Bill You didn't tell your family.

Ron No, I didn't tell them.

Bill Well, you should have.

Ron I don't have to go telling everyone the minute I step out of the house, I'm a grown man.

Bill Could have fooled me.

Ron You don't warn everyone the minute you go round the shops.

Bill Ron, duty free on the ferry to Amsterdam is not popping down the shops.

Ron It was a bet.

Bill I know that.

Ron Which I won.

Bill At what price though, eh?

Ron How many people can say they've played the piano on a cross-channel ferry, eh? How many people can say that, at my age?

Bill You never learn.

Ron I've never even had a lesson.

Bill You put your health at risk, and what for ——

Ron One of those things, Bill.

Bill For the sake of a barman.

Ron He thought I wouldn't do it and I did.

Bill Well, it went wrong then.

Ron No.

Bill Otherwise you wouldn't have ended up where you did.

Ron I was more popular than their paid professional, that's what they didn't like. I had them in the palm of my hand.

Bill You were singing filth, Ron.

Ron Good seafaring material, that's what I was singing. I know how to work a crowd.

Ron You can't sing filth on a public ferry.

Ron I had a damn good try.

Bill Well, you were a fool.

Ron Oh, where's your sense of fun, Bill, you're no fun any more. You could have come with me, couldn't you? We'd have had a wonderful time.

Bill Well, I didn't, did I?

Ron No, but you could have.

Bill (*angrily*) Well, I didn't, so that's that.

Pause

What did it lead to, Ron? You answer that.

Ron I won fifty quid.

Bill You got put in a home.

Ron That's not the reason.

Bill Of course it is.

Ron I had them in the palm of my hand.

Bill If you say so.

Ron They were singing along. I had them, Bill, I had them.

Bill Yeah.

Ron I was in my element, and they didn't like it, they thought I was getting too big for my boots.

Bill I don't know.

Ron Why would they go and do that?

Bill Didn't they ask you to stop?

Ron Well ...

Bill You wouldn't stop.

Ron No. We were having a good time, why would I stop?

Bill They had a right to stop you.

Ron Why?

Bill It's their boat.

Ron I know how to work a crowd.

Bill I know.

Ron Manhandling me like that. Blow to my pride.

Bill You were dealing the blows.

Ron Yes, I was.

Bill What an embarrassment.

Ron Not at all.

Bill Total embarrassment.

Ron I did all right.

Pause

Bill What pianist ever twisted his ankle landing a right hook?

Ron Showing up an old man like me.

Bill You were half cut.

Ron You weren't there.

Bill *You told me.*

Ron You weren't there: you could have been, you could have been there to look after me, couldn't you? See me through.

Bill You were drunk, no one can see to you when you're drunk.

Ron Dutch courage.

Bill You were drunk.

Ron Where were you though?

Bill I was here. Five o'clock spot, remember?

Ron We could have had a five o'clock spot in Holland. You could have been there with me, and I'll tell you something, I'd do it again, ankle and all, I'm not ashamed. I won my bet.

Bill And ended up in a home.

Ron I'm back now, no harm done.

Bill Oh I can't argue with you, Ron; I don't want to argue.

Ron I can do what I like.

Bill I'm not arguing.

Ron We're *discussing*, Bill.

Bill So that you can prove yourself right.

Ron I am right.

Bill If you'd only told him you were going.

Ron No.

Bill Yes.

Ron Well. Maybe.

Bill (*at last*) Thank you.

Ron (*straight away*) But what's it got to do with him? If it's anyone's problem, it's mine, as far as I can see. It's not his business.

Bill Of course it is.

Ron Why?

Bill He's your son for a start.

Ron When has he ever bothered? It's not his problem, it's my problem if I twist my ankle, or sing on boats or try and rob banks blindfold or whatever I choose to do. What's it got to do with him?

Bill He just wants peace of mind, that's all.

Ron Well, we all want that, don't we?

Bill You came off the Amsterdam ferry on a stretcher. He had to take a day off work to drive you home. I don't think you can blame him for being a bit worried.

Ron Worried?

Bill Well of course he was.

Ron (*cleverly*) But he's not worried about *me* is he?

Bill rubs a hand over his face, as if this is all rather too much to take

He's only concerned that I'm going to become a liability. He's worried about *himself*. He's worried about worrying. It's my job to worry. He just wants me off his hands.

Bill Do you think they thought you were trying to prove something?

Ron I was.

Bill To them. That you were fit to live with them?

Ron Don't make me laugh.

Bill Well it's possible.

Ron Live with Arthur and Jean? I wouldn't live in the same county as Jean. She knows that as well as I do.

Bill They're not that bad.

Ron Would *you* live with Jean?

Bill At least there's someone there for you.

Ron There for me.

Bill You're luckier than you know.

Ron They're not there for me, are they?

Bill Oh come on Ron.

Ron Or they wouldn't put me where they did.

Bill You went ——

Ron It's just the insult. They picked me up from the hospital — they took me home, I never said a word. Not one. They came right out with it, there and then. "We're sorry but we can't take you on". I never asked them to take me on.

Bill That's exactly what I'm saying. If you had done, he didn't want to say no.

Ron I never was going to ask that. I wouldn't ask that.

Bill But I'll bet that's not what he thought, that's why he got in first.

Ron Well, he thought wrong.

Pause

It's just the blind cheek of it. We don't think you're safe on your own. We think you should move out. Don't think it's easy for us to say this, they said. What in God's name, after seventy years, makes them an authority on *my* life, that's what I'd like to know.

Bill You can put it behind you now.

Ron I can't, Bill, not after three weeks in there. They bamboozled me, but now I've seen what I'm in for. They've sown the seed of doubt.

Bill Who has?

Ron Arthur and Jean.

Bill They can't tell you to go back. They can't make you.

Ron They did though, they did make me.

Bill Tell them you've changed your mind.

Ron I have.

Bill Tell them.

Ron It's not as simple as that.

Bill They can't make you.

Ron Well, I don't know, do I?

Bill You've said you won't go back, so it's as simple as that. You just have to tell them where you stand.

Ron That's it, though. I don't know where I stand, that's what I don't know. I don't know whether I'm coming or going or what the rules are.

Bill Oh, come on, Ron.

Ron Well it's words Bill, isn't it? It's easy for them, they know it all, they know how to say what they want and make one thing mean another thing, and if *I* say something that doesn't make sense — well, to me it's right.

Bill All right.

Ron (*getting worked up*) It is all right for you because it isn't you. No one's trying to shove you where you don't want to go, but me, they argue left and right and twist their words, but I love my house, I may grumble but I love it. I, you know, I mean *you* know what it means but they don't know. They don't know what it means. (*Beat*) They want me off their conscience. They want me put away.

Bill No they don't.

Ron (*accusing Bill*) I'll end up feeling the guilty one, not them.

Bill I'm on your side, Ron.

Ron Are you, are you Bill?

Bill turns to Ron incredulously

(*Pacified*) Someone's got to be.

Bill They can't do anything.

Ron (*revelling in his own danger*)I don't know what they can do.

Bill You should ask the police.

Ron No, thank you very much.

Bill When it's settled down a bit. They'd know. They could tell you the legal position. Set you straight.

Ron But it's more arguments and words. I don't want all that. I'm simple Bill, simple. Why can't they just leave me alone. It's quite straightforward, I like my fun, but I've always liked my fun. I like the simple things, they give me pleasure. You can't take that away.

Bill No.

Ron Course I'm going to sing on the boat, why shouldn't I? You've got to give it a go. I'm not clever or educated but I give it a go. I'm just simple. And they got me when I was confused, shoving me in there, they got me when I was down.

Bill It was a shock for you.

Ron Course it was.

Bill Yeah.

Ron It was a blow to my pride. I didn't know I was going to twist my ankle, did I? I didn't know I was going to fall.

Bill No.

Ron Course it was a shock. People with less to them than me would have found themselves stuck. I kept the keys to my house so they couldn't sell it. I got out when my head cleared. If you ask me it's them that's out of their senses; I mean nowadays people my age, they go on the Caribbean cruises and all sorts, I know I can't afford that, but I won my bet, didn't I? Yes, I did. I don't know.

Bill sniffs. During the following speech he becomes quite distant, as if the words are washing over him

There'll be a fuss at any rate. From this end. I'll kick up a stink, make a point or two. They have hurt me, putting me through what they have. They are, they're (*mouthing*) shits. All of them. And I never swear without good reason. When he was younger, then it was me that didn't understand: "Dad, you don't understand what I'm going through". Now things have changed, oh yes, now it's him that doesn't understand me: "Oh, you don't understand

me, oh, you don't understand me" ... well, you won't find me
bleating like a lamb.

Pause

Bill I should have been to see you.
Ron Yes, you should have. Have you got a fag?
Bill I don't think I was up to visiting.
Ron Have you got one. A fag, Bill?
Bill No.
Ron *No*?
Bill Not on me, no.
Ron (*after a pause*) Oh. (*He takes a packet of cigarettes from his
     own coat and removes a cigarette from it*) You not smoking, then?
Bill No.
Ron You don't want one?
Bill No.

There is a pause while Ron takes this in and reacts

Ron Why weren't you at church?
Bill (*tired*) I told you.

Pause

   I was in Scarborough.
Ron It was the same usual mess, cars parked everywhere, willy
     nilly, all up the road.
Bill (*distant*) Yeah, always the same.

Pause

Ron Perk up, Bill.
Bill Don't be silly.

Ron Have a fag then.

Bill No.

Ron We might as well celebrate.

Bill (*flaring up*) *Jesus Christ, Ron, I don't want a fag*. (*Calmer*) I'm fine, please just leave me be.

Ron (*indifferently*) Well, don't say I didn't ask.

Bill Don't bully me.

Ron I'm not bullying you, I'm asking if you want a fag.

Bill No.

Ron (*taking a second to reflect*) No, thank you.

Bill No, thank you.

Pause

Ron I didn't really expect you to be here, you're not upset about that are you?

Bill No.

Ron I haven't upset you?

Bill No.

Ron Well, cheer up then, you miserable git. (*He puts the cigarette in his mouth*)

Bill Right, I will have one.

Ron You what?

Bill I will have one. I've changed my mind. I'll have two.

Ron No you won't.

Bill Go on, I'll have a fag.

Ron Not on your nelly.

Bill Come on.

Ron (*replacing the cigarette in the box*) No, I've gone off the idea.

Pause

Bill Suit yourself. The road then, Ron, tell me about that.

Ron What road?

Bill You were talking about the road.

Ron No, I wasn't.

Bill At the church, when there's a service, the church road.

Ron Oh. Well, it's a disgrace, they should do something about it. A church should have proper car parking facilities; it's a joke there on a Sunday.

Bill They can't do anything about it.

Ron They could tarmac it.

Bill It's not theirs to tarmac.

Ron It's in need of repair.

Bill They don't own it.

Ron It's hardly fit to walk on.

Bill Penny Stapleton does.

Ron In gum boots, though, in her great big wellies.

Bill No, she owns it.

Ron Then they should give her the money to do it. You know, what's the point of putting on a pair of smart shoes if they're going to be ruined.

Bill It's part of her land, and if she chose, and bless her she's very supportive, but she needn't let any car up there if she didn't want to.

Ron She can't do that.

Bill If she wants to she can. That's her right as the landowner.

Ron You'd think they would have bought it. So disorganized.

Ron You think what a state the main road would be in if there were no cars allowed up that drive on a Sunday.

Ron And she can do that, can she?

Bill Well she won't, but she could. If it was someone else, then who knows? The only right you have to pass up there in a car, the only time you actually have a right — do you know when that is? The only time you have a right to pass through there in a vehicle is when you're in your coffin.

Ron I don't see why people can't walk.

Bill It's difficult when you're dead.

Ron I just think it's a pity that they can't sort it out; it's a pretty area, and a pretty church, but come Sunday it's a free-for-all.

Bill It's just the outer signs of a general decline, Ron.

Ron Do you think so?

Bill Well, I'll tell you this, right, now after you were put away — em — you know, since we haven't been meeting, I went to Mrs Chapman ... first name, first name, what's her first name?

Ron Mrs C.

Bill I know it, now come on.

Ron Mrs C. That's her name. And I know why.

Bill Well, I went to her son's christening.

Ron Because her real one's awful, that's why.

Bill Ron, I went to her christening.

Ron Well I never got an invite.

Bill No, well is it surprising? You were away.

Ron They knew where I was.

Bill That's not the argument.

Ron makes to speak

(*Cutting over Ron*) The point was they had little service sheets with the hymns and prayers, including the Lord's Prayer.

Ron Oh yes.

Bill Now the priest said he was going to do the 1536 version.

Ron 1539.

Bill Whatever, whatever.

Ron In Latin.

Bill In Latin. And the congregation were going to follow along with the modern version, which was to be printed on the — you know — service cards. But what they printed on the service cards was halfway house between the old and the new, so what the congregation was reading wasn't the new version at all, except those that knew it, and knew that was the one that was supposed to be read.

Ron What?

Bill What I'm telling you.

Ron They should have stuck to the Latin.

Bill But they wanted the modern.

Ron If the church had stuck to the Latin, 1539, then there wouldn't be this problem. The whole point was that you could go into any church in the world, anyone could, and hear the Lord's Prayer, and know exactly what you were hearing.

Bill But people weren't even saying the same one in English. They printed the wrong one on the sheets.

Ron Shambles.

Bill It's a sign of everything that is wrong with the church today. It is very serious.

Ron You're right. And it's the same with the drive. Absolutely ruins your shoes.

A moment. Bill realizes he can avoid the issue no longer

Bill New shoes then, Ron?

Ron Oh — good. You noticed them then.

Bill stares at Ron

   Do you like them?

Bill For me — no. They're not really me.

Ron No, but for me.

Bill (*after a pause*)No.

Ron No?

Bill No.

Ron Oh ... they're a very advanced design.

Bill And you think they suit you?

Ron I find them very reassuring.

Bill Well they look stupid.

Ron wiggles his toes and looks at them

What about your old shoes?

Ron I've moved on from them.

Bill Oh Lord.

Ron You have to throw your lot in with technology, they've made great advances. They understand about feet.

Bill Well there we are.

Ron There we are.

Bill How much, forty quid?

Ron (*waving this away*) Oh no, no, no.

Bill Where's the logic in that, Ron, you tell me.

Ron Sixty. I did have a fall, you know that, and now I'm taking the precaution of counteracting that with grip.

Bill So you break your leg instead of twisting your ankle, do a proper job of it.

Ron (*showing Bill the soles of his shoes*) Look at that. Insurance, for my peace of mind.

Bill You can buy an hour on the Caribbean cruise for sixty quid.

Ron Yeah, well, it's no good if I fall overboard, is it? Now you see there, that panel, that's for circulation. You see, Bill, what they do, they leave small holes to let the air in. And round here they put extra support for the ankles and air in the soles. That's the key feature, you see, for extra padding.

Bill I thought it was grip you were after.

Ron Well, that's it. Support and grip: they're the watchwords.

Bill Sixty pounds for air.

Ron I have to be seen to be doing something.

Bill Why?

Ron Well, I do.

Bill Rubbish.

Ron Course I do.

Bill People will say you are losing your marbles.

Ron They can say what they like.

Bill They will.

Ron They can.

Bill You are losing your marbles.

Ron (*a little sensitively*) No, I'm not. You haven't seen what I have. You'd lose your marbles if you'd spent the last three weeks with me.

Bill Yes, I think I probably would.

Ron In there.

Bill I know. Your shoes don't matter.

Ron I do what I can.

Bill No one's going to be impressed with a pair of shoes. You don't impress me.

Ron No. (*He pauses*) I thought it was the best thing. It was suggested to me by one of the staff at the home.

Bill Well you were misled.

Ron I wasn't forced to buy them, that was my own choice, honestly. They are very comfortable. My friend Jenny liked them. I made a new friend, you know. She suggested it, that's all, and she was the only person that was good to me in there, so I was prepared to listen to some extent, yes. Young girl.

Bill Oh.

Ron Yes, member of staff.

Bill Pretty was she?

Ron Oh yes.

Bill Blonde?

Ron Dark. Very pretty though. Very slim.

Bill Blue eyes?

Ron I don't know, I think so, yes, blue ... She made my bed a few times, helped out with the food, you know, helping in general. Blue-eyed girl.

Bill But she wasn't assigned to you?

Ron No, no, not as such, but she *favoured* me if you see what I mean, because we had something going.

Bill She fancied you, you mean?

Ron We got on like some people do, it's as simple as that. I've got
her address, you know, you have to look out for things that are
going to give you comfort. She used to try and make me go and
sit in the common room, but I would never go. Well. Why should
I have to look at people dribbling. Eh? Why can't there be a
common room where there's not a television on and on all day
with the volume up, and no one understanding a single word, and
shouting out nonsense that spoils it for the rest of us. What's the
point in that? I can't be expected to go and sit in there. So she used
to come up and sit in my room. A quarter of an hour at a time, then
she had to go. I'll get you to meet her. I said to her one day, I said,
"Missie, come here. What rubbish are you serving up today?"
Bill, are you listening to me?

Bill Yes, I am Ron, I am.

Ron It was lunchtime, Bill, lunchtime.

Bill Lunchtime, yes.

Ron And she leant over and said in my ear: "Squirrel sandwiches".

Bill Oh. Well, that can't have been very nice.

Ron We weren't eating squirrel.

Bill No?

Ron No one eats squirrel, do they? It was a joke.

Bill Oh yes.

Ron (*looking for a response*)Ha ha.

Bill (*blandly*) Ha ha, yes.

Ron Well *I* thought it was hilarious and *I* laughed, and that was the
key, you see, because she didn't expect it, she didn't think I would,
and when I did, well, I got such a flash of a smile in return, well,
that made my day. Bill?

Bill I know.

Ron It made my day.

Bill Bright girl, was she?

Ron Oh yes.

Bill I wonder what makes people want to do a job like that.

Ron Well she was only new.

Bill I wouldn't do it.

Ron No, well you're a man. They were nearly all women in there. It's in their blood, I think, caring work like that. Women. Except the chef. He was a man. A quarter of an hour at a time. I tell you, Bill, that was precious, that really meant something to me. You have to see what I've had to go through, I mean ——

Bill Well you're back now.

Ron I don't mind living with older people, don't get me wrong, but I should never have been put with that set.

Bill No.

Ron Never. They were in a bad way ... They aren't people, Bill. They aren't people.

Bill No.

Ron And that gets you down. The common room gets you down, I tell you. I mean how can they arrange a room like that, all the chairs round the outside and not even a carpet. How can they? It's like a doctor's waiting room. Like a bloody doctor's waiting room. I don't want to sit down there, do I, spending all my time looking at someone else, no thank you. I want to be in my room on my own, out of the way. That's all I wanted. And it smells, even if you spray stuff it smells, that's the worst thing, even in my room I couldn't get away from the smell. It gets in your bones.

Bill Let it go now, eh?

Ron That bloody smell.

Bill Let it go.

Ron I'm just trying to get to grips with things.

Pause

Bill I know.

Ron It's getting cold.

Bill Did you tell her?

Ron What?

Bill That you were going to escape?
Ron I think so. I think I did, yes.
Bill It is getting cold.
Ron But I'll phone her.
Bill We can stay for a bit, though.
Ron Oh yes.
Bill I'm glad you're back.

Pause

I missed you. I didn't know what to do.
Ron Stealing. That goes on as well. Pilfering the old people's money, you wouldn't believe it, would you? That's what they do. Who's to know? They think: "Oh, I'll earn myself an easy tenner here and there, nothing too suspicious." People not so sharp as me never realize, and those that do, well, they confuse them with words and say, "No, Mrs So-and-So, don't you remember, you spent that last week on an ice-cream." I had a tenner nicked, *a tenner* — then I got wise. Who would think you can take money from old folk that way? You shouldn't be allowed into that field if that's what you are going to do, but there's no one to stop them, that's the problem. You have to protect yourself. They set themselves up as caring people and then they're allowed free rein.
Bill I don't care, Ron.
Ron I can tell you some terrible stories about the old fogies.
Bill I don't want to hear.
Ron Of course you do. It's funny, some of it.
Bill I don't want to hear.
Ron Then what do you want to hear?
Bill Nothing. I'd just like to sit here.
Ron (*sulkily*) Fine.
Bill No one knows what it's like, do they? No one properly understands.
Ron Some people do.

Bill No one does.

Ron I found someone who did.

Bill You're talking about your girl. You're a bigger fool than I took you for.

Ron She made me happy, Bill, she made me smile.

Bill Well I'm glad someone's happy.

Ron What's wrong with *her* now?

Bill Oh nothing.

Ron Don't begrudge me ——

Bill I don't want to hear.

Ron What *do* you want to hear?

Bill Nothing.

Ron Might as well not talk at all, going on what you say.

Bill That would suit me fine.

Ron You've got to talk.

Bill What's the use?

Ron You've got to.

Bill Well, talk about something other than old cronies.

Ron Jenny.

Bill Or your little floosie.

Ron Like what?

Bill I don't know.

Ron Well, then.

Bill Talk about Catherine and Margaret.

Ron No.

Bill Go on.

Ron It's sad.

Bill No, it's not.

Ron Brings me down.

Bill Why?

Ron They're dead, aren't they?

Bill So?

Ron Brings me down. Don't want to talk about that.

Bill You talk when it suits you.

Ron At the right time, and that's not now.

Bill They're not dead, anyway.

Ron You'd talk about Jenny if you'd met her, you'd talk about the home: it's only natural.

Bill Tell me something good then, make me smile.

Ron I was trying.

Bill Well, go on, then.

Ron She was good, for me, she was what I needed. She smelt fresh, she left her smell in the room, and on my hands sometimes and even on my clothes.

Bill Then you were lucky. You should have stayed where you were.

Ron (*exasperated*) I was only saying about ——

Bill I know, I know, about her. I know what you were saying.

Ron Well, it's all right then, isn't it?

Pause

Bill Don't you feel sad about it? You and a young girl like that?

Ron No.

Bill Like a pervert?

Ron Why should I feel that? There's nothing going on.

Bill All the time getting kicks from a brush of her skirt or a waft of her perfume. That's what it comes down to, isn't it?

Ron No, Bill, I liked her around me.

Bill I know you did. I'd like her around me, but I can't have that, can I?

Ron I liked her looks, all those things, I liked her air.

Bill I'm just jealous.

Ron Well, you can meet her, Bill.

Bill What's the use?

Ron What's that supposed to mean?

Bill (*with distaste*) Sad old man like me hankering after what I can't get? I've still got my self respect.

Ron Couldn't you cope with a young girl around you? Wouldn't you know what to do?

Bill Of course I would.

Ron You're losing your bottle. That's why you never came to
Amsterdam.

Bill I haven't lost my desire, have I, I still function in that respect.
What am I supposed to do with that?

Ron What do you normally do with it?

Bill (*scoffing*) What do I normally do with it?

Ron I know what I do with it.

Bill Yeah, well that's you.

Ron It's natural.

Bill Ah, but does she, Ron, does she know what you do with it? I
bet you don't tell her.

Ron What you don't see doesn't hurt.

Bill *I* can't feel it and pretend I don't.

Ron Well, don't then.

Bill *Don't feel it?*

Ron Don't pretend.

Bill I'd have to. If she thought you or I desired her she'd be off like
a shot.

Ron You make all your own complications.

Bill When was I last looked at? I mean looked at. Never.

Ron I like to look, myself, that's pleasure enough.

Bill What's the use.

Ron It's not sinful.

Bill I want to touch, Ron.

Ron Well do.

Bill (*disgustedly*) Not grabbing knees and clamping my arms
round pretending to be friendly, oh my God, no. No, not that.

Ron I can't help you.

Bill Don't think I don't know that smell you were talking about.

Ron Perfume?

Bill Don't make me say it. The other smell.

Ron What smell?

Bill The nursing home smell, home, what do you think. Of course
I want to smell perfume. Something, I want to smell something:

why do you think I come out here? Something other than my own bloody aftershave all the time.

Pause

I'm sure she's lovely.

Pause

I've been away. I've not been very well. Scarborough.

Ron I know you went to Scarborough, Bill, I'm not deaf, I know what's going on.

Bill Where I had my honeymoon.

Ron (*rattled*) I know that, I know that, I know, I know where you had your honeymoon, I know what you were doing. I'm not that slow.

Bill (*far away*) I was just looking.

Ron What's got into you, Bill?

Pause

Bill Nothing. (*Beat*) Scarborough.

Ron Why? Why d'you go there?

Bill I don't know.

Ron What d'you go back there for?

Bill I don't know ... There I was, that's where I found myself. That's where I ended up. Don't know why, could have been anywhere I suppose; yeah, could have been anywhere. You know Scarborough, Ron.

Ron Course I know Scarborough.

Bill Yeah. The same beach, you know, just the same, just the same. Lovely.

Ron Course it is.

Bill Yeah. (*Pause*) I went to the hotel.

Ron Did you?

Bill I had to, of course — had to look. Couldn't ... and, er ... *The Hillcroft*. You never went in the end, did you?

Ron I don't know, Bill.

Bill *The Hillcroft.* They had a Rolls Royce for taking special guests around the town — you know, like honeymooners. We went in it, a black one it was. Yeah. Mr Capelli, he owned it, the eyetie, you remember, changed his name after the war to "Jones". Capelli his name was. Ring a bell?

Ron I think so, yes.

Bill Well he's dead. They bought him out, some chain — Trusthouse or something and — er — ten years ago: heart attack. Poor bugger. I went in, you know, just to make a few inquiries and — it's changed, yes it has, they've overhauled the *whole place*. I couldn't believe my eyes at first, but of course you'd expect it to change in fifty years. Of course you would. All those little rooms for milling around in, all those armchairs ... It's a restaurant now, the whole lot, one big restaurant, no partitions, nothing. No Roller ... It's posh, don't get me wrong, it's still posh, but ... Oh well ... You know me, I like to be made to feel special. I like people to remember my name. They don't know me for a valuable client, not from the next man. What do they care that I spent my honeymoon in that same building? What do they care what that means to me? Mr Capelli knew our names before we even arrived, he even carried our bags in person. Oh yes. Of course it would change in fifty years, of course it would.

Ron Of course it would.

Bill Of course it would. I walked in, and thought to myself, I'm going to stay here, why not, why shouldn't I? I'll book a room. Once I'd made the decision to stay ... well ... it had to be the room I'd had back then, of course. Had to be. They told me it was unoccupied, but booked. They told me I'd have to have another one. I don't want another one I said, they said "All the rooms are identical" and tried to make out there would be no difference. I started to get hot under the collar. So I said, if all the rooms are identical, then why can't I have the room that I want. "Because, sir, it is already booked". Well, they weren't full, anyone could see that, and I thought, don't you want my custom? They didn't care, they didn't give a monkey's. I said "I'll have the manager".

Ron I hope you stuck it up him.

Bill And this manager, who was supposed to be in a meeting, so they said, came out five minutes later, and it was the same one that had been at the desk, just before. Hadn't been in any meeting at all. Then he thought he'd try and butter me up with a cup of coffee from a percolator in his office. I don't drink coffee, I said.

Ron No.

Bill I said, "I'm British, not French". In the end he wanted to know why I wanted one room and not the other.

Ron And you told him?

Bill Oh yes, I had a field day. I said "Before you were even wearing nappies, young man, this hotel used to be a different place, with clients not businessmen, and an owner not a manager, who wasn't afraid to carry the bags instead of swanning around in his office all day, because he didn't even have an office". I made that bit up. I said, "He used to smoke, *and* carry the bags, instead of wandering around putting up 'No Smoking' notices willy nilly." "That's company policy", he told me. "Don't you have any character of your own," I said, "don't you have any idea of what character is?" If you'd seen this hotel as it once was, then you'd know a thing or two about how a hotel should be run. "Mr Capelli ran this place at a loss", I told him, "and you — you've ruined it."

Ron He wouldn't have liked that.

Bill Well, he'd only been there two weeks.

Ron Is that what he said?

Bill He gave me breakfast for free.

Ron And you got your room.

Bill Yeah. Yeah, I got my room.

Pause

Ron You soft sod.

Bill All that arguing, it was all too much, it took a lot out of me. It took the wind out of my sails.

Ron But you got your room.

Bill I know, I know. But ... (*he shakes his head*) I went in. Can't remember if it was me or the porter went in first. Put my bags down. Heard the door shut. No. I couldn't recognize it. I couldn't recognize it, Ron.

Ron Yes, you could.

Bill I don't know what I was doing back there. I don't know what I was thinking of. All the old furniture had gone, all the old wardrobes and dressers had gone, all the old paintings, the old taps, the bath. All gone. That was my wedding room. My wedding room; very comfortable, I couldn't complain. Could have been anywhere. It wasn't there, Ron, no good, under the papering maybe — somewhere, maybe it went with the wardrobes, I don't know, something had gone. Something. I don't know.

Ron You should never have been there.

Bill Ah, sod 'em, Ron, sod 'em. Went for a walk along the sea front, down on the beach. Freezing it was, wind blowing, plastic bags, standing there, North Sea. Sod you, sod your hotel, Sod your flashy reception and marble, and copycat rooms, sod illness and dying and homes like you were in, eh, sod it, sod it, Ron, sod it. Tests and sodding pills and X-rays. Sod it all.

Ron Bill.

Bill (*running on*) Sod it all.

Ron Don't say that.

Bill I'm tired.

Ron I'm back.

Bill (*under his breath*) Sod it all.

Pause. Ron gets up from the bench

   Where are you going?
Ron Nowhere. (*He walks a little way from the bench and stands*)
Ron What do you mean?
Bill You've got your own way of coping, haven't you? You'll always be all right.
Ron What do you mean "I'll always be all right"?
Bill You've got your new girlfriend for a start.

Pause

Ron She's not my girlfriend.

Pause

   What do you mean?
Bill I don't know, Ron.
Ron Yes, you do.

Pause

   What have you got?
Bill Nothing.
Ron Tell me.
Bill Nothing to tell, Ron.
Ron (*short*) Course there's something to tell.
Bill Nothing to tell.
Ron What are you going on about tests for, and X-rays?
Bill What tests?
Ron You said tests, I heard you say tests.
Bill I haven't had any tests.
Ron What have you got?
Bill Nothing. Nothing.

Ron Are you in pain?

Bill does not answer. Ron slowly goes back to the bench and sits

Have you seen somebody?

No answer

Well?

Bill (*irritably*)No.

Ron If you're in pain you have to see somebody.

Bill Who says I'm in pain?

Ron You have to see somebody.

Bill Who says I want to?

Ron Well you must.

Bill I told you, I don't want to.

Ron They can fix you up, they can do things, they know things.

Bill I'm ill, that's all that matters.

Ron You're ill, you're ill, are you badly ill?

No answer from Bill

(*Angrily*) That's what you've decided is it? On your own, without seeing anyone. That's what you've decided.

Bill That's what I know, Ron.

Pause

Ron But you're going to do something?

Pause

Bill No.

Pause

Ron No. (*His mind is searching for ways to reject this information*) Come on, Bill, I need a bit more than that.

Bill Why?

Ron I don't know, proof ... What about the doctors? They can do something for you.

Bill I'm not going to see any doctors. No one is going to make me do anything other than what I want to do, not you or them or anybody. No one. It's my right, if I choose, to do what I want.

Ron But if it hurts, Bill ——

Bill Yes it does hurt, so what if it does, so what?

Ron Then get drugs, see someone for the pain.

Bill I'm not going to some hospital.

Ron You don't even know.

Bill I'll have the last laugh ——

Ron On what?

Bill On whatever it is.

Ron You don't even know. (*He pauses; doubtfully*) Do you? (*Quickly*) Everyone knows you can fight against these things.

Bill If you want to.

Ron Jenny could help you.

Bill Maybe.

Ron She will.

Bill That's not what I want though.

Ron Not what you want?

Bill No.

Ron You don't want help?

Bill No.

Ron Blimey Bill, I don't know.

Bill Please, Ron.

Ron I don't know what to say.

Bill Don't say anything. Why don't you take my word for it? Why won't you listen to what *I* say?

Ron I don't know what you're saying.

Bill I want to die properly.

Ron What's properly?

Bill I don't know.

Ron There you are then.

Bill Just properly.

Ron You don't know what you're saying.

Bill I do.

Ron You've just said ——

Bill Like an animal.

Ron What?

Bill It's my right.

Ron What right?

Bill To die. I don't know, to crawl away and die, that's what they do isn't it? I don't know ——

Ron I don't know, Bill.

Bill That's what they do. Not to be searched out, or found, or rescued or treated. They go to the long grass, don't they? That's what they do.

Ron There isn't any long grass.

Bill There's no shame in that. No shame at all. That's me, Ron, dignified. I'm not a hanger-on.

Ron Don't sound so pleased with yourself.

Bill It's off my chest, isn't it.

Ron That's no good, it doesn't help me.

Bill You'll be all right.

Ron No, I won't.

Bill You're always all right.

Ron Do yourself in, then.

Pause

Bill When the time comes.

Ron My God, Bill, that's terrible. That's never my way ——

Bill (*warningly*) Ron.

Ron Well, *suicide* ——

Bill *No. Please.*

Ron I have to ——
Bill I'm happy.
Ron The five o'clock spot, Bill.
Bill I can't. You've got your Jenny.

Pause

Ron Yeah.
Bill You have.
Ron Yeah.
Bill Haven't you?
Ron Yeah, I have.

Long pause

Bill, make me a promise. Will you — will you promise me — if
you can get here — then get here. Do you see that? Do you
understand me? You get here. Five o'clock spot. Until you can't.
That's all I want to know. Have you got that? You get here. (*He
pauses*) You're a stupid bugger. You know that, don't you?
Stupid bugger, you stupid bugger, what about a drink? I want a
drink. You wear me out, Bill. Are you coming for a drink, are you
coming for a pint?
Bill (*pause to think*)If you're buying.
Ron Well, come on then.
Bill Wait on a moment.
Ron Come on.
Bill Not yet. (*Pause*) In a while.
Ron It's cold, Bill. Gone right through my coat.
Bill Just a little longer.

The Lights slowly fade to a dim blue light

Bill exits. Ron sits on the bench

The Lights slowly come up on Ron alone on the bench. He sits for some time, then lights a cigarette

Black-out

CURTAIN

FURNITURE AND PROPERTY LIST

On stage: Park bench

Personal: **Ron**: packet of cigarettes, matches

LIGHTING PLOT

To open: General exterior lighting

Cue 1   **Bill**: "Just a bit longer."   (Page 33)
            Fade to dim blue light

Cue 2   **Bill** exits   (Page 33)
            Bring lights up slowly to general
              exterior lighting state

Cue 3   **Ron** lights a cigarette   (Page 34)
            Black-out

EFFECTS PLOT

No cues